ULTIMATE
College Basketball
Road Trip

By Jeff Seidel

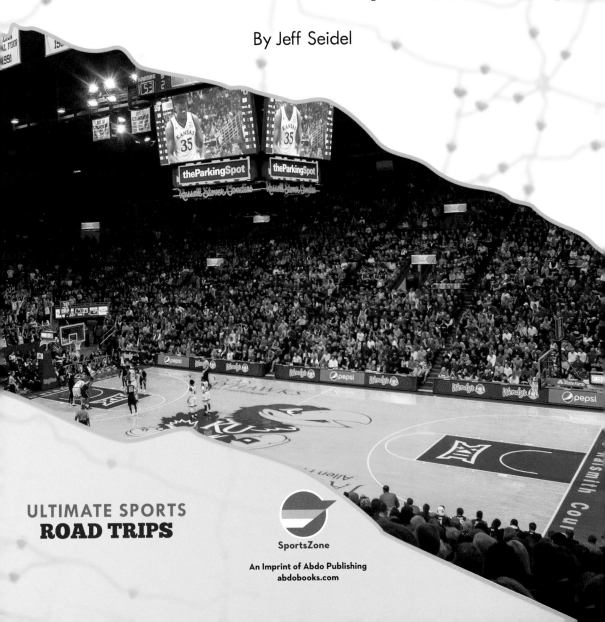

ULTIMATE SPORTS
ROAD TRIPS

SportsZone

An Imprint of Abdo Publishing
abdobooks.com

ABDOBOOKS.COM

Printed in the United States of America, North Mankato, Minnesota
092018
012019

THIS BOOK CONTAINS
RECYCLED MATERIALS

Cover Photo: Nick Tre. Smith/Icon Sportswire/AP Images
Interior Photos: Nick Tre. Smith/Icon Sportswire/AP Images, 1; Jeff Moffett/Icon Sportswire, 4–5; Jeff Gross/Getty Images Sport/Getty Images, 7; John W. McDonough/Sports Illustrated/Getty Images, 8–9, 10, 44; Janis Schwartz/Shutterstock Images, 13; Reed Hoffmann/AP Images, 14; David Eulitt/The Kansas City Star/AP Images, 16; Kirby Lee/AP/Newscom, 19; Brian Spurlock/USA Today Sports/Newscom, 20; iStockphoto, 23; Michael Reaves/Getty Images Sport/Getty Images, 24; Jeff Roberson/AP Images, 26–27; Lance King/iStockphoto, 29; Gerry Broome/AP Images, 31, 36–37, 45; Kevin C. Cox/Getty Images Sport/ Getty Images, 32; Kelly vanDellen/Shutterstock Images, 35; Sara D. Davis/AP Images, 39; Howard Smith/ USA Today Sports, 41; Bill Streicher/Icon SMI CCP/Newscom, 42

Editor: Bradley Cole
Series Designer: Melissa Martin

Library of Congress Control Number: 2018949179

Publisher's Cataloging-in-Publication Data

Names: Seidel, Jeff, author.
Title: Ultimate college basketball road trip / by Jeff Seidel.
Description: Minneapolis, Minnesota : Abdo Publishing, 2019 | Series: Ultimate sports road trips | Includes online resources and index.
Identifiers: ISBN 9781532117503 (lib. bdg.) | ISBN 9781532170362 (ebook)
Subjects: LCSH: Sports arenas--Juvenile literature. | Sports spectators--Juvenile literature. | Basketball-- Juvenile literature. | College sports--Juvenile literature.
Classification: DDC 796.323630--dc23

TABLE OF CONTENTS

INTRODUCTION
TIP-OFF! 4

CHAPTER 1
PAULEY PAVILION 6

CHAPTER 2
ALLEN FIELDHOUSE 12

CHAPTER 3
ASSEMBLY HALL 18

CHAPTER 4
RUPP ARENA 22

CHAPTER 5
DEAN SMITH CENTER 28

CHAPTER 6
CAMERON INDOOR STADIUM.......... 34

CHAPTER 7
THE PALESTRA 40

MAP 44   ONLINE RESOURCES. . . 47

GLOSSARY. 46   INDEX 48

MORE INFORMATION. . . 47   ABOUT THE AUTHOR . . 48

Tip-Off!

The ultimate college basketball road trip will be an amazing journey showcasing history, rowdy fans, beautiful arenas, and great tradition. It will show off some of the best college athletes in the country and celebrate with body paint and crazy student sections. Some arenas will be small and compact, whereas others will be among the biggest in college basketball. Fans will get loud as players hit game-winning shots.

The journey will take us to the East Coast and sunny Southern California, along with multiple stops in America's heartland, where kids might grow up playing basketball in barns that look a lot like smaller versions of today's arenas. There will be dunks and heckling. Scoreboards will light up as players streak across the hardwood playing for their schools. These are the best spots to watch college basketball.

Student sections help create the great atmosphere in college basketball arenas.

PAULEY
PAVILION

At Pauley Pavilion, the University of California, Los Angeles (UCLA) Bruins became the first perennial powerhouse of college basketball. UCLA dominated college basketball in the 1960s and the first part of the 1970s. The arena opened the summer before UCLA's 1965 season, and the team still plays there.

Much of the fame of the building can be tied to the many legendary players who wore the UCLA uniform. Kareem Abdul-Jabbar played in the first game ever at Pauley Pavilion on November 27, 1965. At that time, players could not compete on the varsity team until they were sophomores. Abdul-Jabbar—then known as Lew Alcindor—suited up with the freshman squad. They beat the varsity team 75–60. Things only got better from there.

Coach John Wooden's teams played eight of their 10 national championship seasons at Pauley. The Bruins even posted an astounding 88-game winning streak. In fact, UCLA had a home record of 149–2 at Pauley from 1965 to 1975. That is a big reason

EDWIN W. PAULEY PAVILION

Los Angeles, California

Date Opened: June 11, 1965
Capacity: 13,800
Home Team: UCLA Bruins

 UCLA's success can be seen hanging from the rafters at Pauley Pavilion.

why there are 11 championship banners hanging from the rafters.

Wooden built a dynasty in Los Angeles. Wooden coached his

last game at Pauley Pavilion on March 1, 1975. The Bruins beat

Stanford 93–59. UCLA won its 10th national title a few weeks after

that, and Wooden retired from his job.

The latest renovation has changed the way things look in the
building. The court where the stars of past UCLA teams played
was finally replaced after 47 seasons. New scoreboards, improved
seating, a widened concourse, and the new Wooden Way along
the eastern concourse updated the arena. Wooden Way pays

tribute to the history of UCLA basketball. The wood paneling in Wooden Way is from the Pauley Pavilion's original court. A statue honors Wooden and three cabinets hold memorabilia from the program. There is so much history that the mementos have to be changed out.

The court at Pauley Pavilion is called Nell and John Wooden Court. UCLA wanted to honor the great coach and his wife with the new court. Wooden stayed connected to the program and the building long after his retirement. He came to most UCLA home games and sat behind the bench. The seats in the arena are blue, except for Wooden's honorary gold seat.

 John Wooden's influence at UCLA can be seen all over Pauley Pavilion, including on the court that bears his name.

Beyond preserving history at Pauley Pavilion, the remodel added modern updates too. The university added an electronic ribbon board around the arena, additional screens for fans to watch the game from the concourse, and more bathrooms. The concessions received upgrades as well. Fans can choose from Subway, Jamba Juice, a coffee house, and a pizza parlor. There are even food trucks on the south side of the arena.

> ## FUN FACT
> Pauley Pavilion hosted men's and women's gymnastics in the 1984 Olympic Games that were based in Los Angeles. The men's team won the team gold medal with three UCLA athletes on the squad.

Pauley Pavilion also has hosted a number of big-name non-sports events. Prince Philip of the United Kingdom visited for a ceremony in 1966. The final presidential debate between George Bush and Michael Dukakis in 1988 was at Pauley. Jay-Z and Rihanna played there in 2009.

Pauley Pavilion has always been a building where winners play. UCLA has 40 national titles in various sports in this building, including men's and women's volleyball and gymnastics. But the building will always be known for basketball first.

ALLEN
FIELDHOUSE

Fans attending a game at Allen Fieldhouse will undoubtedly walk away with many memories of the game. One of them will likely be of "Rock, Chalk, Jayhawk!" echoing in their ears.

The school's famous chant comes from a cheer that a chemistry professor made up for the University of Kansas science club in 1886. He used "Rah, Rah, Jayhawk, KU." But the "Rah, Rah" section of the chant somehow was changed to "Rock Chalk." Chalk Rock is the name of a limestone outcropping found on Mount Oread, where the Kansas campus is located. The two words were switched around and the most famous chant in college basketball was born.

In fact, President Teddy Roosevelt said it was the greatest college chant he'd ever heard. The King of Belgium asked for people at the Olympic Games in 1920 to give an American college yell. The athletes did the "Rock Chalk" chant. The famous chant is only a part of the Allen Fieldhouse experience.

ALLEN FIELDHOUSE

Lawrence, Kansas

Date Opened: March 1, 1955
Capacity: 16,300
Home Team: Kansas Jayhawks

 Legendary Kansas coach "Phog" Allen helped make Kansas basketball the powerhouse that it is today.

The building was named for Dr. Forrest Clare "Phog" Allen. He was the basketball coach at Kansas for 39 years. The University of Kansas opened Allen Fieldhouse on March 1, 1955. Kansas beat

Kansas State University 77–66 in front of a crowd of 17,228 that day. The school estimates that since the 1964–65 season, more than 5 million people have attended Kansas games in "the Phog."

Kansas knows that basketball is an important element of the student experience. KU students are a major part of Jayhawks basketball. More than 4,000 seats are reserved for students at each game. Many of those seats are close to the floor. The fans are a big reason that Allen Fieldhouse is considered one of the greatest places for college basketball games. Longtime Kansas coach Bill Self said he gets "goose bumps" every time he walks through the tunnel and onto the court.

FUN FACT

A banner at the north end of the building reads: "Pay Heed, All Who Enter/Beware of 'The Phog.'" The original was painted by a group of Kansas students in 1988 and hangs there still.

Fans often line up from the Kansas locker room area to the court. They begin cheering for the Jayhawks before the game starts and do not stop until after it's over. The fans never hesitate to show how much they care for their team. And KU players love it.

Self said that the loudest he's ever heard the building was during the 2012 Border War game. The Border War is the rivalry

game between Kansas and the University of Missouri. Facing conference rival Missouri, Kansas's Thomas Robinson blocked a shot to force overtime. Then Kansas rallied to win the game 87–86. That was the last time Kansas and Missouri met as conference rivals, because Missouri switched conferences the following season.

Kansas players often stay to sign autographs for the numerous fans that remain after the game. It's a way of paying back the people who make Rock, Chalk, Jayhawk the success it's been for decades.

The Border War games at Allen Fieldhouse have had plenty of big moments over the years.

3 ASSEMBLY HALL

The state of Indiana loves basketball. And excited fans of the Indiana University Hoosiers have packed Assembly Hall since the first game there. Since that time, the Hoosiers have had a lot of home-court success in Assembly Hall.

The often-animated Bobby Knight won three national championships at Indiana. Knight also won 11 regular season conference championships as head coach of the Hoosiers. He won 659 games on the Indiana sideline between 1971 and 2000. He became a legend both for his success and his outbursts at officials.

FUN FACT

The renovation to the building includes five new monuments that pay tribute to Indiana's national championship teams from 1940, 1953, 1976, 1981, and 1987.

But Assembly Hall is known for more than just Knight. Indiana had some impressive winning streaks there through the years. The Hoosiers have the most recent undefeated season in major

SIMON SKJODT ASSEMBLY HALL

Bloomington, Indiana

Date Opened: December 18, 1971
Capacity: 17,222
Home Team: Indiana Hoosiers

 Assembly Hall's unique design makes it stand out among college basketball arenas.

college basketball. In 1975–76 Indiana went 32–0 and won the

national championship. Even when the Hoosiers are having a

down year, their court is a dangerous spot for opposing teams

to play. In 2011 Indiana's Christian Watford made a last-second three-point shot that gave the unranked Hoosiers a 73–72 victory over No. 1 Kentucky.

Assembly Hall is also known for having a bit of an unusual design. Athletic director Paul Harrell did not want the building to have a "circular-bowl design." He wanted it to be different than the arenas at Illinois or Purdue. Harrell wanted the seats to be like a pair of theater sections that faced the same stage. The building also has very steep stairs in the lower tier.

Philanthropist and Indiana graduate Cindy Simon Skjodt gave the school a $40 million gift that helped renovate the arena. Indiana updated the main entrance and added club-level seating. Fans can now watch the game from the upper concourse as well. With a new scoreboard in place, the old one is now used as a decoration in the south pavilion. Center court was also saved and now hangs in the north pavilion. Simon Skjodt Assembly Hall was reopened and dedicated on October 14, 2016.

FUN FACT

The 1976 Hoosiers team was the last undefeated national champion in men's college basketball.

4

RUPP
ARENA

Adolph Rupp grew into a legend both at the University of Kentucky and throughout college basketball. He coached the Wildcats from 1930 until 1972. His teams posted a record of 876–190 during that time. The Wildcats made the Final Four six times with Rupp as the coach and captured the national championship four times. That post-season success was a big reason why the school named the arena it built in 1976 after him.

FUN FACT

The NCAA men's Final Four was held in Rupp Arena in 1985. Villanova upset Georgetown for the national championship in one of college basketball's biggest surprises. One year later, Rupp Arena hosted both the SEC Tournament as well as the women's Final Four.

The building opened at the beginning of the 1976–77 basketball season and has grown into one of the most famous college basketball arenas in the nation. It also has played a big role in Kentucky remaining a national power for long after Rupp's era.

RUPP ARENA

Lexington, Kentucky

Date Opened: October 7, 1976
Capacity: 20,500
Home Team: Kentucky Wildcats

 Rupp Arena combines history with modern amenities and technology.

The Wildcats have won nearly 90 percent of their home games since Rupp Arena opened. Coaches Joe B. Hall, Rick Pitino, Tubby Smith, and John Calipari each had championship seasons in Rupp Arena.

The seating is split into two main areas. The lower level consists of 10,000 seats with cushions like those often found in a theater. The upper level features metal bleachers that can hold up to 10,000 more fans.

The arena underwent a $16 million upgrade during the 2015–16 and 2016–17 seasons. The highlight of the renovation is a 34-by-28-foot (10-by-8.5-m) state-of-the-art video board. Even the air ducts were painted Wildcat Blue in Rupp Arena. After the 2018–19 season, the seating capacity was lowered from 23,000, and chair-back seating was added to some of the upper-deck sections. This dropped Kentucky from the second-largest to sixth-largest arena in college basketball.

FUN FACT

For the fan experience at Rupp Arena, ice cream has grown very popular. During the 2017–18 season nearly 3,500 ice cream cones were sold at each Kentucky home game. The ice cream cones have even been mentioned on ESPN.

A lot of work and technology go into creating an interesting experience for University of Kentucky fans. For example, the Wildcats do a lights-out introduction of players, which includes a video along with indoor fireworks. Other updates that work toward a better fan experience include new electronic ribbon boards, new high-definition video boards in the corners, and a new speaker system.

The fans return the effort put into Rupp Arena by making it the loudest indoor arena in the world. When No. 2 Kansas played

 Coach John Calipari, *second from left*, has helped Kentucky put on a great show for fans every game.

No. 4 Kentucky on January 28, 2017, a representative from the Guinness Book of World Records measured the sound. The Wildcat faithful set the new record at 130.4 decibels.

With John Calipari at the helm, Kentucky basketball has put on a show on the court as well. Through the 2017–18 season Kentucky had posted five straight seasons of at least 26 wins and deep postseason runs.

5

DEAN SMITH
CENTER

University of North Carolina at Chapel Hill (UNC) has long been one of the toughest places for visiting teams to play basketball. Carmichael Arena opened in 1965, and North Carolina finished with a 169–20 record there before moving to the Dean E. Smith Student Activities Center during the 1985–86 season.

The Smith Center bears the name of North Carolina's Hall of Fame coach. Dean Smith tormented other teams in both of UNC's home arenas. Smith took over in 1961 and coached the Tar Heels for 36 years. They won 879 games and two national championships under Smith. Those 879 wins place Smith fourth in career coaching wins.

Tar Heels fans often call the arena "the Dean Dome." Its capacity places it among the five biggest college basketball arenas in the United States. Smith did not initially want the building to be named after him. But when the university said it would be best for the basketball program, he accepted. In the first game ever played

DEAN E. SMITH STUDENT ACTIVITIES CENTER

Chapel Hill, North Carolina

Date Opened: January 18, 1986
Capacity: 21,750
Home Team: North Carolina Tar Heels

there, his unbeaten and top-ranked North Carolina edged out rival No. 3 Duke University 95–92 in a nail-biter finish.

Many big-name musical acts have played at the Dean Dome. Phil Collins, Bruce Springsteen, and the Grateful Dead are among the older groups who have performed there. Future President Barack Obama held a rally there before the 2008 election. He made sure to fit in by wearing a Carolina Blue tie, much to the delight of the 18,000 in attendance.

Prior to the 2016–17 season the behind-the-scenes areas of the Dean Dome were renovated. Donor lounges and areas for eating team meals, hosting recruits, and player scouting were renovated. Many of the walls were decorated in murals of past players or program statistics. One of the lounges has a mural that depicts Michael Jordan. There is even a wall that showcases Jordan shoes that were specially made for the Tar Heels.

One criticism of the building is the lack of noise. The Carmichael was known for how loud it could get. That noise really

FUN FACT

North Carolina center Warren Martin scored the team's first basket in the first game at the building off a pass from Kenny Smith, now a basketball analyst on TNT.

The Dean Dome's home-court advantage has helped the Tar Heels post a lot of wins over the years.

went up when playing rivals Duke or Maryland. But that noise was often missing in the early years of the new building. Architects took a look at the arena's design to enhance the crowd's cheering.

The Dean Dome was built with two levels and no suites or club level seating. So in 2000–01, a standing-room-only section just for

students was added behind the baseline by the North Carolina bench. The section holds 200 students. The addition helps fans make more noise, especially when opposing teams are shooting at that end of the court—as if playing against the legendary UNC Tar Heels wasn't difficult enough. UNC coach Roy Williams enjoys the extra noise and atmosphere the additional fans provide.

North Carolina students fill a standing-room-only section to help make the Dean Smith Center even louder.

6 CAMERON
INDOOR
STADIUM

The noise at Duke University's Cameron Indoor Stadium makes it one of the toughest places to play in college basketball. Visiting teams encounter Duke students painted blue and white, dressed in all kinds of outfits, and screaming as loud as they can in an attempt to bother the other team. Cameron Indoor's relatively small capacity still has the power to create quite a ruckus. Duke fans enjoy making noise.

Despite its small size, the stadium was considered large when it opened in 1940. Yale University had recently built a basketball gym that seated only 1,600. Duke aimed high with its new arena. Now, its compact size

FUN FACT

Students camp out for long stretches to get tickets for games. There can be up to 100 tents lined up by the arena for students to stay in while waiting for tickets.

CAMERON INDOOR STADIUM

Durham, North Carolina

Date Opened: January 6, 1940
Capacity: 9,314
Home Team: Duke Blue Devils

 The Cameron Crazies are some of the wildest and most entertaining fans in college basketball.

is considered part of its charm, as fans are squeezed in shoulder to shoulder. Construction of the arena took only nine months.

When Duke opened its new arena against Princeton, the arena was just named Indoor Stadium. The school changed the name in 1972 to honor its longtime athletic director and basketball coach, Eddie Cameron. That same day, unranked Duke faced

archrival University of North Carolina, then ranked third in the
nation. Senior guard Robby West made a late jump shot to give
the Blue Devils a 76–74 victory. There have been many big games
for the Blue Devils in Cameron Indoor too. During the 2005–06
season, point guard Sean Dockery hit a half-court shot at the
buzzer to beat Virginia Tech.

The energy from the student section is just as intense as the actual game. The students at Cameron Indoor have earned a reputation for mocking and teasing opposing teams. For example, some students liked to wear rubber skullcaps to impersonate Maryland coach Lefty Driesell when the Terrapins came to town. When former Kansas coach Roy Williams took over at North Carolina in 2003, Duke fans had something special for him too. They dressed up as characters from *The Wizard of Oz* so Williams would realize that he was not in Kansas anymore. Such antics helped the Duke student section earn the nickname the "Cameron Crazies."

FUN FACT

The basketball court was renamed "Coach K Court" and the area that is outside the arena is known as "Krzyzewskiville," or simply "K-ville," in honor of the longtime coach.

Some of the greatest college basketball players of the past 30 years have made Cameron Indoor their home. Christian Laettner, Grant Hill, J. J. Redick, Shane Battier, and Carlos Boozer, are just a few that have played for Duke. The Blue Devils have sent many players to the National Basketball Association (NBA).

Cameron Indoor Stadium may be small, but it serves as a classic home for a program that has become one of the most prestigious in the nation. The Blue Devils won five national championships between 1991 and 2015. Mike Krzyzewski coached the team for all of them. Cameron Indoor remains a place that teams do not look forward to but that any basketball fan wants to see.

Cameron Indoor has been a pipeline of NBA talent, with players such as J. J. Redick playing for the Duke Blue Devils.

7

THE PALESTRA

Tom Izzo has been the coach for the Michigan State men's basketball team since 1995. The Spartans won a national championship, made seven Final Fours, and played in most of the best basketball arenas in the United States. But Izzo had never coached a game in the Palestra, the legendary basketball arena in Philadelphia.

FUN FACT

During afternoon games, skylights on the Palestra's roof can allow the sun's rays to reflect onto the court.

Penn State coach Patrick Chambers hadn't coached at the Palestra either. Chambers wanted to play a game there too. So Izzo and Chambers worked out all the details. On January 7, 2017 Penn State defeated Michigan State, 72–63 at the Palestra.

The Palestra seats a relatively small number by today's standards. But 8,700 fans made a pretty big crowd when it opened back in 1927. It sits on the campus of the University of Pennsylvania

THE PALESTRA

Philadelphia, Pennsylvania

Date Opened: January 1, 1927
Capacity: 8,722
Home Team: Pennsylvania Quakers

 The Palestra might be older and smaller than many arenas, but many great basketball games have taken place on its court.

and remains busy, especially during the Penn Quakers' basketball season.

Because the court sits below street level, the arena looks very small from the outside. It is easy to drive right past the 33rd Street entrance without noticing it. Many seats do not even have chair-backs, but fans can find a good view of the court from anywhere in the arena.

Penn plays men's and women's basketball there. It also hosts volleyball matches and wrestling meets. In fact, the school says that the Palestra has hosted more games and more visiting teams than any other building in the nation.

The Palestra's fame grew as it became known as the host of some epic battles between Philadelphia's "Big 5" schools. Penn, La Salle, Villanova, St. Joseph's, and Temple formed an unofficial "conference." They played a round-robin against each other for bragging rights among the city's top basketball programs.

Penn still plays its home games at the Palestra. One of the many great games happened before the shot clock era. On January 16, 1969, Penn faced city rival No. 9 Villanova. The Quakers held the ball for more than three minutes before Steve Bilsky hit a 25-foot shot at the buzzer. That gave Penn a 32–30 victory.

The Palestra remains so beloved that many visiting NBA teams practice there when in town to face the Philadelphia 76ers. Just like Izzo, they simply want to experience the historic Palestra.

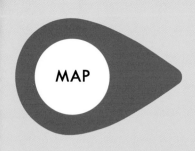

MAP

1. **Edwin W. Pauley Pavilion.** Los Angeles, California
2. **Allen Fieldhouse.** Lawrence, Kansas
3. **Simon Skjodt Assembly Hall.** Bloomington, Indiana
4. **Rupp Arena.** Lexington, Kentucky

WA

MT

OR

ID

WY

NV

UT

CO

CA

1

AZ

NM

5. **Dean Smith Student Activities Center.** Chapel Hill, North Carolina
6. **Cameron Indoor Stadium.** Durham, North Carolina
7. **The Palestra.** Philadelphia, Pennsylvania

Glossary

baseline

The out-of-bounds line underneath each basket, along the short sides of the court.

fieldhouse

A building enclosing a large area suitable for various forms of athletics and usually providing seats for spectators.

Hall of Fame

The highest honor a player or coach can get when his or her career is over.

perennial

Enduring or continually recurring.

renovation

The process of restoring or updating the physical conditions of a building.

retire

To end one's career.

shot clock

A clock that counts down the number of seconds remaining before a basketball team must shoot the ball.

three-point shot

Any shot taken behind the three-point line.

More Information

BOOKS

Ervin, Phil. *Total Basketball*. Minneapolis, MN: Abdo Publishing, 2017.

Silverman, Drew. *Indiana Hoosiers*. Minneapolis, MN: Abdo Publishing, 2014.

Silverman, Drew. *Kansas Jayhawks*. Minneapolis, MN: Abdo Publishing, 2012.

Online Resources

Booklinks
NONFICTION NETWORK
FREE! ONLINE NONFICTION RESOURCES

To learn more about college basketball arenas, visit **abdobooklinks.com**. These links are routinely monitored and updated to provide the most current information available.

Index

Abdul-Jabbar, Kareem, 6
Allen, Forrest Clare, 14
Allen Fieldhouse, 12–15
Assembly Hall, 18, 21

Bilsky, Steve, 43
Border War, 15–17
Bush, George, 11

Cameron, Eddie, 36
Cameron Crazies, 38
Cameron Indoor Stadium, 34–39
Carmichael Arena, 28, 31

Dean Smith Center, 28–33
Dockery, Sean, 37
Driesell, Lefty, 38
Duke University, 30, 31, 34–38

Harrell, Paul, 21

Indiana University, 18–21

Jordan, Michael, 30

Knight, Bobby, 18
Krzyzewski, Mike, 38, 39

Obama, Barack, 30

Palestra, 40–43
Pauley Pavilion, 6–11

Robinson, Thomas, 17
Roosevelt, Teddy, 12
Rupp, Adolph, 22
Rupp Arena, 22–26

Self, Bill, 15
Simon Skjodt, Cindy, 21
Smith, Dean E., 28

University of California, Los Angeles
  (UCLA), 6–11
University of Kansas (KU), 12–17, 26, 38
University of Kentucky, 21, 22–27
University of North Carolina (UNC),
  28–30, 33, 37, 38
University of Pennsylvania, 42–43

Watford, Christian, 20
West, Robby, 37
Williams, Roy, 33, 38
Wooden, John, 6, 8–11

About the Author

Jeff Seidel has been a journalist in the Baltimore-Washington area for more than 30 years. He lives there with his wife, two children, and two very faithful cats.